THIRST NO MORE: A WOMAN'S JOURNEY TO REDEMPTION

Yvette Wilson Bentley

A Parishioner's Perspective Series

Yvette Wilson Bentley

©2015 Yvette Wilson Bentley

All rights reserved. Except for use in the case of brief quotations embodied in critical articles and reviews, the reproduction or utilization of this work in whole or part in any form by any electronic, digital, mechanical or other means, now known or hereafter invented, including xerography, photocopying, scanning, recording, or any information storage or retrieval system, is forbidden without prior written permission of the author and publisher.

The scanning, uploading, and distribution of this book via the Internet or via any other means without permission of the publisher and author is illegal and punishable by law.

Purchase only authorized versions of this book and do not participate in or encourage electronic piracy of copyrighted materials. Your support of the author's rights is appreciated.

Any group or organization listed is for informational purposes only and does not imply endorsement or support of their activities or organization.

For ordering, booking, permission, or questions, contact the author.

ISBN 13: 978-0-9961327-0-1
Library of Congress Control Number: **2015905172**

Published by Wryte Type Publishing, Inc.
Printed in the United States of America

Cover Design:	Lloyd DeBerry, Fine Art & Graphics
	www.fineartandgraphicsdesign.com
Editing:	Shantae Charles, God Ideas, LLC
	www.godideasllc.com
Typesetting:	Yvette Wilson Bentley, Words 2 Life, LLC
	www.words2life.com

Yvette Wilson Bentley

Dedication

*I dedicate this book to **Mary F. Snardon,** my other mother, who always lets me know what I can be rather than remind me of what I was.*

Yvette Wilson Bentley

INTRODUCTION

Almost always, I keep paper and pen within my reach. Yes, we live in the 21st century and have electronic devices – cell phones, tablets, etc. - I own a few of them. Nevertheless, when it comes to God-inspired thoughts, I like experiencing the humility reverence as I am writing them down. I am not distracted with the mechanical functions of a device. I can look down at a journal page or a piece of paper and see what God poured into me.

When I take pen to paper, I enter into private instruction with God. He is guiding and instructing me how to use the gift that He gave me – the gift to write. God's instruction is like no other. It is a mode instruction beyond human power. It can only come from the Divine One.

Whenever I am at Sunday School or worship service, I have paper and pen. If I heard the teacher or a student share something inspiring in Sunday School, I am jotting it down. I do the same thing in worship, except I am jotting down things that I have heard the preacher share during his sermon. When I read back over what I have written, I am amazed. So many times I have written down the exact message that I needed to hear. I have written down messages that God led me to share with others. Sometimes, I create brief posts and share them on social media and my website.

God is leading me to pen a number of books that will compile into a series. These books will be based various Scriptures and how they parallel with my life's experiences. By no means do I claim to be anyone's theologian. I am simply sharing from a Parishioner's Perspective, which is the name of the series.

THIRST NO MORE: A Woman's Journey to Restoration is the first book in the series. This book is based on one of my favorite Bible stories. It wasn't difficult to write this book but I learned a valuable lesson. I learned that no matter how long you have been saved, you will always have an area in your life that can only be restored and healed by the power of The Living Water.

You don't have to take my word for it – feel free to try it for yourself!

Table of Contents

Chapter One	11
Chapter Two	18
Chapter Three	24
Chapter Four	30
Chapter Five	36
Chapter Six	42
Chapter Seven	49
Chapter Eight	56
Chapter Nine	63
Chapter Ten	68
Connection Through Reflection Exercise	81

Yvette Wilson Bentley

CHAPTER ONE

A TYPICAL WOMAN WITH UNTYPICAL TENDENCIES

Whether it's on the job or in the home, some people say that "A woman's work is never done." Some people will agree with the statement whereas others will strongly oppose

There are women who contend whether it is in the workplace or at home, "work is work." There is little evidence of women being employed during Biblical times like women are today.

Nonetheless, those women had plenty to do. Cooking, cleaning and tending to their families was all in the name of "woman's work." They didn't have running water, so they drew water from a well to manage household tasks.

In the Samaritan community, most women traveled together to the well around the same time every day. They also used this time to have some "girlfriend" time and discuss matters that were important to them. I believe they made good use of their limited time. Once the women returned from the well, they dispersed back to their respective homes. Unless there was some sort of scheduled event taking place, they probably didn't see each other again until the next morning.

The women went out in the early morning hours when the sun was relatively cool. On occasion, a few women traveled for an evening draw before nightfall. They laughed, chattered and helped one another as they made their way to and from the well.

There was a woman from Sychar that

appeared to be a loner. Like the other women, she traveled to the well daily; however, she didn't travel at the same time as the other women nor did she travel with them – she traveled alone.

She did not engage in the camaraderie with the other women. She traveled at high noon - the hottest times of the day. Over the years, she had been married five times. Presently, she was unmarried and living with a man.

It appeared that the community did not find favor with her carnal lifestyle. It seems that they looked upon her as an outcast. I can envision the repeated laughter and negative comments coming from the other women. Nonetheless, the lone woman chose to avoid others by traveling to the well at a different time of day.

These women may have seen themselves as "typical" women, or a "strong example of something" (Webster's 2004). As a group, they seemed to share a bond and other commonalities. It appears the lone woman has been excluded from the group of other women. Also, it's possible that the other women perceived her to be

an "untypical" woman or someone who is "not representative or characteristic of a particular type, person, etc. (www.dictionary.com).
Having had five husbands and living with another man while unmarried was not what the women considered as the "norm."

These women seemed to live by the old creed of "birds of a feather flock together." I believe the women looked at the lone woman as a "bird of a different feather." Her behavior was contrary to theirs. It appeared she was not considered as "one of them" and they wanted nothing to do with her.

Have you ever found yourself labeled as an outcast? Was it because of your actions? Has your behavior ever gone from being typical to untypical? Let me be the first to answer that yes, mine has.

I spent almost 20 years of my life living a double life. I had two sets of friends and lived two different lifestyles. The first lifestyle was built on morals, values, education, vocation and faith in God.

My other lifestyle was forever-changing. There were alcohol, drugs, sex, nightclubs and a meaningless romantic relationships. I crossed so many boundaries that I believed both lifestyles to be one and the same.

On the surface, I appeared to be doing the "right" thing. By my teenage years, I crossed the line. I became a teenage mother. I was drinking alcohol and using drugs. During most of my 20s, I did the "normal" things. I went to work, ran a household and was a wife and mother.

We did family stuff on Saturdays and attended church on Sundays. I hung out with friends who led similar lifestyles. For years, things appeared to be fine. It's always calm before the storm.

In a four-year period, my life went from being an occasional thunderstorm to a destructive tornado. I brought harm to everyone and everything I came in contact with. Things happened I didn't think would happen. My husband and I divorced. I was in the clutches of a domestic violence relationship. I got strung out on drugs. I spent time in jail. I was evicted from my home. I lost custody of my son. I lost my job. I lost the respect of my family and friends. Last but not least, I lost all hope and respect for myself.

I never thought that "living from pillar to post" would become my reality – but it did. I never thought that I would become a "crack head" – but I did. I never thought I would think about taking my own life – but I did. I was sinking in quicksand. I had no idea how I got to where I was and not a clue of how to get out.

I had become an outcast. My friends stopped taking my calls. There were a few that would tell me how disappointed they were in me and hang up the phone. Who could blame them? I had not been raised to live like I was living. I asked a couple of friends if I could stay with them. They told me no. They didn't want me coming around.

I couldn't believe they wouldn't help me. They knew I had a problem. I had the nerve to be angry with them. The truth of the matter is that it would have been impossible for anyone to help me. Why? I hadn't done anything to help myself. I looked for everyone else to do for me what I needed to do for myself.

It was easier to point the blame at everyone else than to accept responsibility for my own mess. I needed to get up off my behind and do something about it! The reality of knowing I had burned all my bridges with family and friends is the lowest feelings I have ever had.

Can you relate? Have you ever felt like an outcast? Take the time to ask yourself some questions. Search within yourself. You may discover some of your own outcast tendencies. When I took the time to examine myself, I came to terms that society did not make me an outcast; I did a fine job of doing that to myself.

As you search within yourself for the answers, ask God for courage to help you to face what you find and how to use it for His will.

CHAPTER TWO

JESUS GETS THIRSTY, TOO!

The New Testament illustrates many accounts of Jesus ministering to others: Jesus raising Lazarus from the dead (John 11) and when He helped the man into the healing pool of Bethesda (John 5). In Matthew 26, we find one of Jesus' most memorable acts of ministry when he shared the Last Supper with His Disciples. Also, there is the story of the woman with the issue of blood (Luke 8). There are many other accounts; these are a few that came to mind.

During the time Jesus lived on earth, he lived as a flesh-and-blood man. Though He is the Son of God and one-third of the Holy Trinity, he got thirsty like any other human being. Jesus and the disciples had done a great work during their stay in Judea (John 3). Once their work was done, Jesus decided to head back to Galilee. But He needed to go through Samaria (John 4:4). His "need" to go through Samaria was not due to personal pleasure or peer pressure. The common route would have been to go northwest through Jericho and then cross the river Jordan. Jesus did not strike out and do things on his own – He prayed and waited on direction from the Father before pursuing his next task or assignment.

As the disciples ministered together with Jesus, they also traveled together. However, this particular trip was different. By the time they reached Samaria, He sent them away to buy food. He knew why the Father had sent Him to Samaria. He also knew what the Father sent Him there to do. This assignment was designed solely to be carried out by Jesus Himself rather than him and the disciples.

When He arrived in Samaria in the noon hour, he was hot, tired and thirsty. So he sat next to

Jacob's Well. When the Samaritan woman saw Jesus, it's possible she thought why was this man there and what did he want. The story doesn't indicate that she knew who He was on first sight. If she did know who Jesus was, do you think she would have acted differently? She could have either did her best to make a good impression or allowed her shame to convince her to hide from Him and miss a blessing.

Think about this: You meet a man at the grocery store. You think that he's going to ask you for a dollar. You find out that he doesn't want a dollar but He is the Son of God. Would you act differently? I would! I would be trying to give Him a dollar and everything I own. After all, this is The Messiah! What else needs to be said?

It looks like all this woman wanted to do was draw her water and leave. So whoever this stranger was and whatever his problem was – it was *his problem* and not hers! Or so she thought.

Nothing beats some cold water on a hot summer day. My grandmother used to have a tin pitcher and cup set. When you put cold water in one of those cups that water stayed cold all day. Who remembers packing ice cubes in a Mason jar and filling it up with water? Yes, I like a cold soft drink or even some Kool-Aid sometimes. At the end of the day, though, cold water will always be my first choice.

One hot summer day, I was on my way home from work. I stopped at a neighborhood restaurant to pick up dinner. It was 105 degrees outside. It was hot enough to fry an egg on the sidewalk. I waited in line to place my order. A gentleman with long gray hair walked up to the service window and asked for a glass of water. The cook told him a glass of water would be $1. The man told him that he had his own cup. The cook told him no again. Then the man asked could he get some water out of the restroom. Again, the cook refused the man and then threatened to call the police if he didn't leave the building. The man did as he was told and left the restaurant.

I ran outside trying to catch the man. I wanted

to give him $2 to get water from the store on the next corner. By the time I got outside, the man was nowhere in sight. I even walked down to the store to see if he was there. Again, he was nowhere in sight. I became angry. Here it was, 105 degrees, and a human being was refused a drink of water! The man had his own cup. Would it really been an inconvenience to let him fill his cup up and leave?

What happened to people practicing the Golden Rule: *Do unto others as you would have then do unto you?* Is that a lost art in the 21st century? At 105 degrees, how in the world could someone refuse any living creature a drink of water?

Then I thought about what I have been taught: no one knows the day nor the hour when Christ will return. We need to be careful how we treat people. We could be face to face with the Master at any given time. That restaurant cook could have been in the presence of Jesus Christ and not have had a clue!

Hebrews 13:2 says "Be not forgetful to entertain strangers: for thereby some have entertained angels unawares." Last, he missed out on an opportunity to bless another human being. When it comes to blessing others, you do not have the right to "pick and choose" who you will bless and who you will not.

The woman may have looked at Jesus and asked herself, "Who does he think he is?" First, he's a Jew that shows up in Samaria – their tribes do not get along. Second, he is talking to her alone in public without her husband being present. That's against the law. Last, why does he think he's different?

In the natural sense, that's all she could see. However, the supernatural Christ was there to extend a Divine invitation to drink of Him, The Living Water.

Chapter Three

I Can't Be Seen Talking to You!

Jesus encountered people from all walks of life. As lovely as it would be for the whole world to "get along" with each other, that's not the way things work. There are those people who get along; then there are those who don't. For those that don't get along, the exchange can be either pleasant or unpleasant. People can come with all sorts of reasons why they do not associate with those from other groups.

For example, one group may feel other groups come from the "wrong side of the track." They come from different races or religions. If the "green" people don't like the "blue" people and the "green" girl gets caught talking to the "blue" boy, it's going to cause problems between the groups.

Jesus kept the "main thing the main thing." He focused on His mission and His purpose. He knew the woman was a Samaritan and he was a Jew. That was a irrelevant. He was also aware of the bad blood that ran between the two tribes. It all began when Assyria conquered Israel. Most Samaritans were forced to live in Assyria and the five alien tribes took up Samaria's former residence in Israel (see 2 Kings 17: 13-34).

As time went on, Samaritans returned from Assyria and began intermarrying within the five tribes. By the time Jesus came along, they were no longer considered to be authentic descendants of great Jewish ancestors. Their religious beliefs had been mixed rather than been of true Judaism. Jesus chose to disregard the dissension between the two tribes. (He was the Worship. He was the shadow of what they were fighting over).

Here are a few questions that may have crossed the woman's mind: Should she stay and talk to this man? Should she leave and act like she never saw him? If she does talk to him, will somebody see them? After all, it wasn't customary for any man, let alone a rabbi, to hold a long conversation with an unfamiliar woman in plain sight.

Since I have been sober, I had to learn to change "old people, places and things." It didn't make sense to me at first. It took a little while for that to sink in. It was a big and bitter pill to swallow. It was scary at first. I was scared I would lose something. I thought I would lose my friends and no longer be accepted. Up until age 32, I did most things for people to accept me.

"Trust in the process." That was another parable I often heard. I didn't understand it but thank God for the courage to trust it anyway. Life used to be fun. After 21 years of my life had spanned, I was hopeless and desperate. The pain had become too great. Was it worth holding on to? No, it wasn't. So God helped me let go of what I thought I was losing, only to find it wasn't worth holding on to in the first place.

After being sober a little over a year, a friend let me borrow her car. I went to church and planned to go to a 12-step meeting afterwards. On my way to the meeting, I stopped at an old friend's house. My plan was to say hello, use the restroom and be on my way.

For the 10 minutes I was there, there wasn't any smoking or drinking going on. Nonetheless, the chaos, excitement and confusion was in high gear. It's time to go!

I got to the car and it wouldn't start. I panicked! Oh, my God, what are people going to say when they find out that I'm down here? My girlfriend is going to kill me. I knew I shouldn't have come down here. If somebody sees me, they will think I've gone back to doing what I was doing! After about an hour, my girlfriend arrived with the tow truck. I've been rescued!

Being rescued did not come for free. I had to endure the lecture my girlfriend had waiting on me. She let me have it! She lectured me about the danger I had placed myself in. Then she painted a graphic picture of all that could have happened by going to an "old playground with old playmates," even it was just for a few minutes.

Normally, I would have blown her off. As much as I wanted to, I couldn't. I knew she was right. Just knowing what could have happened shook me up enough to know that I wouldn't be talking that chance again.

We have to ask God to show us who we should be connected to. There are times that I don't have to ask God about a person; He equips me to make decisions. The very people I try to overlook or discount are the ones God appoints me to be a part of my life. Then there were those I thought were a blessing, only to find their only agenda was for them to win and me to lose. Those people have no place in my life. Now those are the people I don't want anyone seeing me talk to. They mean me no good. God didn't send them. He does not maintain what He didn't ordain. There's only one thing to do when those type of people approach you - RUN!

It appears she has no idea that Jesus is The Son of God. Like most women, she appeared to be curious. It seems she didn't have a clue about what she would discover. Yet, she was determined to learn as much as she could about this man.

Trust God. Take His hand and travel beneath your surface. It will be an amazing experience!

CHAPTER FOUR

TAKING IT ALL IN

Many scholars have coined the conversation between Jesus and the Samaritan woman as Jesus' longest recorded conversations. What a privilege to have a conversation with Jesus! She thought she was talking to just another Jew. She had no idea this conversation would forever change her life.

Have you ever heard the old saying, "Never judge a book by its cover?" Well, it wouldn't be hard to find her guilty of that. All she saw was a hot, tired man who wanted a drink of water. She seemed irritated about him asking for water.

"Will you give me a drink?" He asked (John

4:7).

"How is it that You, being a Jew, ask a drink from me, a Samaritan woman?" (John 4:9).

"If you knew the gift of God and who it is that is saying to you 'Give me a drink,' you would have asked him, and he would have given you living water." (John 4:10). This was Jesus' answer to her question. Was this the answer she expected?

The woman tells him, "Sir, you have nothing to draw with and the well is deep" (John 4:11). But then it appears that two words were resonating with her - living water. "Where can you get this living water?" she asked. "Are you greater than our father, Jacob, who gave us this well and drank from it himself, as did also his sons and his livestock?" (John 4:12).

Jesus explains that everyone that drinks the water from the well will be thirsty. However, if they drink the water that He gives them, they will never be thirsty again. The water that He gives them will become a spring in them, welling up to eternal life (John 4:13-14).

It's easy to look in the wrong direction for satisfaction. I was miserable for years because I sought outside of myself for something or someone to make me feel complete. I tried to quench a thirst I was not equipped to handle. It became a vicious cycle of insanity – trying the same thing, expecting different results. I had premeditated resentments. I had expectations and when they didn't go my way, here comes the resentments! I didn't realize I was a thirsty person. Thank God for knowledge and understanding.

The Samaritan woman asked Him for some of the Living Water and where was it. She didn't want to go down to the well anymore (John 4:15). She had suffered socially for many years as an outcast. Her suffering spread out amongst the entire community with both men and women. I believe it's safe to say that she had grown tired and weary of the treatment she had received from the community. If there was a way for her to put her suffering to an end, she needed to know. She did not want to go down to that well anymore.

Unbeknownst to her, she was about to learn the difference between flowing water and The Living Water.

If I had been engaged in that same conversation with Jesus, I would have perceived Living Water exactly as she did. At first, she did not grasp the "meat" of the statement: "Indeed, the water that I give them will become in them a spring of water welling up to eternal life." She missed the point that Jesus was making and was clueless that He was there to bless her.

Have you ever missed out on a blessing because you didn't listen or follow instructions? What about killing a blessing before it has a chance to materialize?

Some years ago, a friend called me about a position her company was hiring for. She told me that she would get me a interview if I wanted one. Since she was the Human Resources Manager, she was able to put me at the top of the candidate list. She described the job and then advised me of the application process. Once that was completed, I would be called for an interview.

The interview was scheduled for the next week. I had one time to make a first good impression. I arrived for the interview twenty minutes early. "To be early is to be on time and to be on time is to be late." The interview went great. "You'll be hearing from us within the week," was the last thing the manager said as I was leaving her office.

I knew I had that job in the bag! I gave that interview everything that I had. I couldn't think of one single reason why she wouldn't hire me.

As promised, I got a phone call the following week. It was not the news I was looking to hear. My friend, called to let me know that I didn't get the job. I was confused. I thought everything went well. As a friend of mine says, I thought that "check was in the mail."

After several minutes of listening to me whine, she told me that I did not follow the directions of the application process. What directions? I was supposed to take a typing test. I didn't recall anything about a typing test. Nonetheless, since I failed to listen to all the instructions, I lost out on a great opportunity.

Later in life, I realized my selective-hearing is a by-product of my mindset. As far as I was concerned, taking a test didn't apply to me; therefore, I didn't bother to retain the information. I blew it. When you don't follow directions, you miss out. I thought I was bigger than the rules. All my thinking got me was a "Thank you for applying; however, we have decided to move on with another candidate" letter.

God loves us so much! He allows us another opportunity to either get it right or make it right. He does not penalize or chastise us for what we don't know. We can't know what we don't know. Once we are enlightened with knowledge, then it's time to say goodbye to our excuses. This doesn't come instantly or easily. We have to practice this daily. When you don't know, you don't know. But once you know better, then do better.

Ask God to rid you of your selective hearing so you can take in all of what He has to say to you!

Chapter Five

In Spite of Ourselves

"You can't teach old dog new tricks." "A leopard can't change its spots." "I'm too old to change."

Do you think the Samaritan woman would agree with either of those statements? They are pretty are strong societal beliefs. Those that agree would probably say, "Well, I guess what they say is true."

Hold up! Wait a minute! You're not a dog! Surely, you're not a leopard! Lastly, as long as you have breath in your body, there is always an opportunity a chance to change!

The Samaritan woman has been ridiculed, judged and condemned by her peers based on her lifestyle. It appears the woman had little, if anything, to say in her own defense. Silence is consent. If we have been labeled by someone and don't speak up, it appears we agree with what have penned us to be.

Nobody has to succumb to silent assent. Ask God for courage and strength to stand boldly. Ask Him for the confidence to speak faith in words and demonstrate it through your actions the truth of who you are.

According to John 4:4, Jesus had the need to go through Samaria so he could bless the woman. He has the *need* to reach out to you at your crossroad. At your crossroad is where you, the empty bucket, meets the Living Water. He needed to be there. Jesus had penciled this woman into his schedule. She had a date with Divine Destiny.

During the "dark" years of my life, I had to face one of the most shameful things I have ever done: stealing money from my grandmother. It was indeed a sin and a shame. She was the one person in the world that gave me *anything* I asked her for. The fact that I had stolen from her was too much for her to fathom. Anyone that knew my grandmother could tell you that she would not hesitate to "get you told" when the need arose. Well, this definitely was a time to get me told, but because she was so upset, this was a time that was the exception to the rule. She decided to send her son, aka my father, to handle the situation. Trust me when I tell you, there was nothing nice or pretty about that confrontation – nothing at all.

I began looking at my life. How did I get here? How did I become so far-removed from life? There were things that I did not have to do. They were solely based on choices I made. Through it all, God loved me, protected and directed me into a new way of life.

When I started on my recovery journey, I was told to take things one day at a time. I looked up one day and ten months had passed. It was also my grandmother's 81st birthday. A party with dinner, cake and ice cream would be held at her home with family and friends later that day. I was still feeling guilty about having had taken her money and was trying to come up with a reason not to go. My father must have sensed it. When I talked to him that morning, he told me that he would see me there and hung up the phone. I knew that was not an invitation, a suggestion, nor a choice. Daddy had spoken.

I was nervous when I walked into the house. This was the first time I had seen my grandmother in about a year. I didn't realize that time had passed since the last time I had seen her. But there I stood, ten months sober and working on being a better person. She grabbed me, we hugged each other and we cried.

I made amends to her for stealing her money. I offered to pay her back. She told me changing my life was payment enough - the Lord had answered her prayers. No, she was not happy about what I did. She told me Lord had forgiven me, she had forgiven me and it was time for me to forgive myself. I promised her that I would. We then joined the others in the dining room for dinner and dessert.

By the time I left her house, I was hoarse from laughing so much. I am so thankful that I didn't allow fear to keep me from going to my grandmother's house that day. Look at what I would have missed out on! It was one of the most memorable days I had with Grandmommy that I will always cherish.

In Samaria, men and women did not converse publicly unless their spouses were present. Jesus was aware of that when he asked the woman to go fetch her husband. She was truthful and told him that she didn't have a husband. It was at this point that Jesus began to tell her about her whole life. She didn't seem to be prepared or expecting to have this conversation with a complete stranger. I don't believe that she expected Jesus to tell her about her whole life, including her five ex-husbands and the man she was living with yet not married to.

She had been exposed! By telling this woman her whole life story, Jesus exposed her sin. There are people who would have ridiculed and condemned a person further for their sins. That was not Jesus' intention. He intended to awaken her dormant conscious so she could experience redemption and restoration. He intended to fill her empty bucket with The Living Water. There was only one thing that he required of the woman. She had to repent. By repenting, she received forgiveness and a bucket full of The Living Water.

Jesus bestowed His unmerited grace and mercy upon her as He has done for us. In spite of herself, He deemed her worthy to receive His favor.

The same thing that Jesus required of the Samaritan woman is the same thing He requires from us today. If we want to receive His forgiveness, we must repent. Once we repent, He forgives. He loves us just that much. Isn't that good to know?

That's all I need to know.

Chapter Six

Can't Live Without Him

Have you ever decided you didn't need help from anyone? "It's just me against the world." "I can make it on my own." "I don't need anybody." "I came into this world by myself and I will leave here by myself."

I used to agree with those type of statements. It was hard for others to get through to me when I had my mind locked on that mode of thinking. Sometimes I can be stubborn which doesn't always work in my favor. Being unwilling to change my mind is not always a good thing.

Whenever I acted like I didn't need anyone and I could do things on my own, I was actually throwing temper tantrums. Things weren't going my way. People were not doing what I wanted them to do or doing what I think they should be doing. When it came to people not doing what I wanted, I viewed everyone equally – there were no favorites. It could be anyone from parents, children, spouse, a co-worker, a supervisor or even someone at the grocery store. Eventually, I had to face facts.

Not only did not getting my way was not working, it wasn't getting me anywhere at all. I had pushed people away, thinking I could live on my own. Through a few trials, I found I couldn't live in this world alone like I thought I could. When the trials became intense and the struggle became real, I no longer wanted to be a solo act. I was convinced I needed people to make it.

How long did it you to realize that you cannot walk the path of life on your own? Did it take you days, weeks, months or years? I know there are those that grasped that right away. Then there are those that it takes them longer than others. Hopefully you reach a point of surrender.

Do you remember the day when you realized you can't live life by yourself? Do you know that in order to win, one must surrender? I tried everything I knew to have peace. I ended up spiritually bankrupt. When you surrender, God lifts you up out of your huddle of complete defeat. You are covered and protected. He will supply all your need. You will be able to do all things through Him. Your life will never be the same.

The Samaritan woman said that she "perceived that he was a prophet" (John 4:19). She knew there was something different about Jesus. No, she did not know that Jesus was the Son of God and part of the Holy Trinity; however she figured that He was a spiritual being that should be acknowledged and revered.

Like the Samaritan woman, I once thought that it was too late to change my life. I was convinced that my life would only get worse. Between the harms I had caused others and my revolving tours in and out of jail, I was convinced that I had reached the point of no return.

I thought that I was either going to overdose, get murdered or go to prison. God, however, didn't see it that way. That's because He had a purpose for my life. On September 18, 1996, I'd had enough – I was done. I couldn't take it anymore. I was too scared to live and too scared to die. I contemplated suicide. I couldn't stab myself – couldn't stand the sight of blood. I was too scared to shoot myself. I didn't have any poisonous pills to take. I quickly realized that suicide was not an option. There was only one thing left for me to do. I got down on my knees out and cried out that three-worded prayer, "God help me" and cried like I never have before.

When I got up from the floor, both my mind and spirit were renewed. I was ready to get help. My mother had told me where to go and what to say when I got there. There was nothing left to figure out. I knew my mother would not send me in the wrong direction. So, it was time to put the plan that she gave me into effect. In less than 24 hours, I walked into the place that landmarked my new beginning. I had no idea how this new-way-of-life-deal was going to work. I believed that whatever it came along with, it had to be better than what I had been doing.

Did I think I could do it? That was the first question. I didn't think so, not at first. I didn't think that I could change. I felt truly hopeless. I was scared of "slipping on the banana peel" back into my old ways. I was even more scared of others seeing me slip. Like the Samaritan woman, I was an empty bucket. I was tired and dehydrated. The rubber had met the road.

I wanted something different but I was full of fear. God sent people to help me walk through the fear. Slowly, my thinking began to change. I started feeling hopeful and empowered. I stopped condemning myself and starting believing that, "Yes, I can do this!"

"Did I *want* to do it?" That was the second question. The first question was about my ability. This question related to my willingness. This was not a snap decision to make. I had to give serious thought about living a different life. This meant changing my actions. I needed to be sure that whatever I decided, I could live by the decision.

I used to think that life wasn't nothing but a party. I thought my old way of life was fun. Then the day came when I realized it wasn't fun anymore. I had crossed that invisible line. I had to take complete inventory of my life. There were painful and ugly things I had to face about myself. What once was fun became a necessity. I had hurt a lot of people. I almost destroyed myself. I even discovered a few good things hidden behind my defects that never had a chance to shine. Having the courage to look at myself gave me the confidence to start liking myself. I liked the relationship I was forming with God. This new life was far better than the life I had before.

God told me: "Yvette, if you keep living like you have been, it's because you want to. The new life I have for you is better than you can imagine. All you have to do is trust Me."

My spirit began drinking God's words. I became saturated with His Living Water. My bucket was no longer empty. I have thirsted no more. That was over eighteen years ago.

In the eyes of Christ, it's never too late. He's always ready to receive us, forgive us and restore us. I tried living my life before without Christ. Living on my own will was unsuccessful and almost fatal. I wasn't even living - I merely existed.

It wasn't until Christ filled my empty bucket with His Living Water that I knew what it meant to be alive. I no longer wanted to exist. It's time to live!

CHAPTER SEVEN

TRUE WORSHIP

Is there a right or wrong place to worship God?

With such a wide variety of religious and spiritual preferences, answers will vary. There are people that attended church. Others worship privately in their homes via television, radio or Internet broadcasts. There are also others who engage in worship groups.

Is it wrong to worship in any other place than a church building?

The Samaritan woman made reference to her ancestors having worshipped in the mountains (John 4:20) but the Jews claimed the people must now worship in Jerusalem. Little did she know, she was about to find out the meaning of true worship.

In John 4:21, Jesus enlightens the woman about worship by explaining the following: *"Jesus declared, 'Believe me, woman, a time is coming when you will worship the Father neither on this mountain nor in Jerusalem.'"*

Most Sundays, our family went to church. As children, we did not get the option of whether or not we wanted to go to church – we went. On Saturday night, you got your clothes together, got your hair pressed and you took your bath. We left home at 9:00 a.m. sharp and worship service started at 11 a.m. Sunday School started at 9:30 a.m.

When it comes to where and when to worship, there are those who believe they are right, others are wrong and vice versa. Our main focus should be worshipping the Father. Focusing on whether to worship here or whether to worship there is irrelevant. We are to worship Him anywhere and everywhere! Amen!

Hebrews 10:25 teaches us that "We are the Church, not the building." Therefore, there is no right or wrong place. One place is no better nor worse than the other. God does, however, place emphasis on coming together with others to worship: You Samaritans worship what you do not know; we worship what we do know, for salvation is from the Jews (John 4:22).

For years, I paid attention to each and every single sermon that I have heard preached; yet, I wouldn't open my Bible to read the Scriptures. I felt like I didn't need to. The preacher would read the Scripture and then preach about it. There was no need for me to remember it. All I had to do was pay attention to the message and I'd have it! WRONG!!!

One day, I heard the preacher say, "Don't take my word for it; read the Scriptures for yourself." That wasn't the first time I had heard the preacher say it. Whenever I would hear it, I would blow it off. In the past, I wasn't mature enough to understand the discipline and commitment that I needed to follow the directions. Now I was ready to experience change in my relationship with Christ and my worship.

Once I began studying the Scriptures, I

understood why I was worshipping. I was familiar with attending worship – I had been going to church all of my life. However, I was clueless when it came to being a worshipper. Being a worshipper, a true worshipper, is one who is committed to God in mind, body and spirit. That's what I strive to be today. In some ways, I understood how the Samaritans were worshipping what they did not know (John 4:22).

The Samaritans worshipped the Lord but they also worshipped other gods and idols (see 2 Kings 17:28-41). For a long time, I worshipped lifestyles. I worshipped "stuff & things." I worshipped romantic relationships, money, drugs, prestige, false sense of importance and the list goes on.

I thought salvation was something I was entitled to because I said, "I believeth!" Thank God for knowledge. Knowledge is power.

I remember worship services on Sunday mornings. The choirs would be singing, the preachers would be preaching and the people, would be shouting, "Thank you, Jesus," "Praise the Lord," "Glory to God" and the like. One of the biggest shouters was my mother. I was about five years old the first time I heard her shout. It scared me so bad that I started crying.

Later, I asked her why she was shouting in church. She said that she was shouting because God had been good to her. I was confused. If God was so good, why did people do all that screaming and hollering? Did it really take *all of that?* And why were people crying?

One Sunday, I asked my grandmother why people shouted in church. She told me that was just the way that some people worshipped the Lord. I asked a few more questions. As usual, she laughed and told me I asked too many questions. She told me one day I would understand. I still didn't understand but I took her word for it anyway.

I have been blessed to live long enough to understand what my grandmother was talking about. The things she used to tell me about Jesus when I was a little girl now make sense. I am thankful to draw from those lessons on loving and serving the Lord.

Jesus explained to the Samaritan woman that God is a spirit. He seeks true worshippers that will worship Him in spirit and in truth. "I know that the Messiah (called Christ) is coming. When he comes, he will explain everything to us," said the woman to Jesus (John 4:25). This statement that the woman just made is not to be taken lightly. She is not one that practices religion as the other in her community, yet she has religious knowledge. Her statement illustrates two important attributes – faith and hope. She has faith that the Messiah is coming and hope His explanations will provide the community with everything they need.

"Jesus said to her, 'I who speak to you am He'" (John 4:26). Say what? She had been conversing with this man, only to find out that He was The Christ. Wow! How would you respond if you were in that woman's shoes? I thought about it; I thought of several scenarios and they all ended with me fainting on the floor. This verse put me in mind my mother used to tell me: "Be on your best behavior at all times – you never know who you will run into."

My mother and all those other people that I would hear shouting on Sundays were worshipping in spirit and in truth. It is amazing to know that. It's even more amazing to have an understanding of that for myself.

When Christ revealed Himself to me for the first time, it blew my mind. Do you remember the first time that Christ revealed Himself to you?

I strive daily to be the best I can be. I don't do it perfect; some days are better than others. I am learning not to be hard on myself when I don't hit the 100% mark.

As long as my worship is honest, sincere, loving and most of all true, there is no right or wrong way to worship The Lord Our God!

CHAPTER EIGHT

I'VE GOT TO TELL IT!

Communication is how people beings relay information to one another. Modern times affords an assortment of methods and devices to communicate: social media, texting, cell phones and video messaging. We also use television, newspapers, writing, telephones, verbal communication and last but certainly not least, nonverbal communication (93% of communication is non-verbal).

Over the years, society has transitioned into different eras of communication tools and skills. A person that is "tech-savvy" gives meaning to "multitasking. " They can post on Facebook, send a text message, have a conversation on Skype, write an email and tweet on Twitter simultaneously from two or more devices. Using one device or platform at a time works just fine; thank you very much.

When modern technology works, it is a beautiful thing. When it doesn't work, it can be a difficult, inconvenient, unpleasant and even unattractive experience.

During the Biblical days, the only options to communicate were verbal, nonverbal or written. When information or messages needed to be communicated, people traveled from house to house or either gathered together, i.e. during a worship service.

The Samaritan woman had just engaged in the most incredible experience of her life. What was supposed to be a normal trip to the well had turned into a divine encounter. She had met the Messiah. He granted her deliverance and salvation through The Living Water. She was restored from her old self into a new person. Without haste, she leaves the water pot and heads to town. She tells everyone to come to see this man who told her everything about herself.

"Could this be the Messiah?" So the other Samaritans went to see what this woman was talking about (John 4:28-30).

Has God been so good to you that you can't keep it to yourself? I'm talking about that kind of *good* when He has made a way out of no way? When He has blessed you and showered you with His favor? He's been that good to me, more than once.

I once applied for a job and had to have a background check. The employer called me a few days later and told me I had legal issues that needed to be addressed. I had outstanding criminal charges and there was a bench warrant with a cash bond for my arrest. I almost fainted. I had done so much dirt when I lived "in the dark" that I didn't remember anything about the situation.

A friend connected me with an attorney who agreed to take my case. After meeting with him, I was scheduled for court the following Friday morning. The bench warrant was withdrawn, which alleviated the fear of wondering if the police were going to stop me or pick me up and cart me off to jail. I did my best to remain positive but I was a nervous wreck. The night before court, I got down on my knees. I told the Lord that I did not want to go to prison. I then asked Him that if going to prison was His will for me, please help me accept it and keep me from losing my mind. Thy will be done.

I arrived at the courthouse an hour before court began. I was *not* taking a chance on being *one second late* for court. The last thing I needed was to go to jail for contempt of court for being late. I had enough to deal with. One of my best friends met me there (thank God). We went in the courtroom exactly at 9 a.m. When we were seated, I looked around and didn't see my attorney. I started panicking. My friend told me to calm down – he would be there.

Twenty minutes later, my attorney walked in the courtroom with the biggest smile on his face. Why is he smiling? I could be losing my freedom and he's smiling. Yes, I was tripping. He leaned down and told me that everything was going to be just fine. I didn't know what that meant. My friend told me, "Girl, he's got you – stop worrying." Finally, I began to calm down.

A few minutes later, the bailiff called my name. My attorney escorted me to the judge's bench. The judge read off my charges, aka, my "list of shame" as I hung my head. After she finished reading the charges, the unbelievable happened. The prosecutor said the Commonwealth has decided not to prosecute the case. I wanted to say, "Could you repeat that please? I don't think I heard you." He shared with the judge that I had completed a residential treatment program, was gainfully employed, a part-time college student and a community volunteer.

I wanted to ask him was he sure he was referring to the right person. Here was the prosecutor giving me all these glowing remarks. True enough, I had accomplished the things that he told the judge. However, one may have thought he was recommending me for a job because his attitude was so positive and upbeat. The judged dismissed all the charges. She then agreed to expunge the charges from my record within five years if I didn't get any new charges. I walked out of the courtroom a free woman!

I know that was nobody but God that made that happen. I called everyone I knew to tell them what He had done for me. I wanted everyone to know how He blessed me with His favor. God came through for me - I couldn't keep that to myself! It may have appeared that the judge let me walk out of that courtroom. Some may even think that it was the prosecutor that got me off the hook. What I know about God is He will use anybody He chooses to fulfill His will without their knowledge or permission. By chance, if they did know that God was using them, it wouldn't matter. As a friend of mine says, "God will make a liar tell the truth one time for His purpose!"

I understand the Samaritan woman's urge to go tell others about "that man." Girl was on a mission! She dropped her pot and headed to town with a sense of urgency. It was imperative for her to tell the others what she had experienced.

I feel a sense of urgency to share new and unexpected experiences with others for two reasons. First, we are commissioned to share the Good News (see Mark 16:15). In simple terms, we are to tell our story and share our experiences. Second, we have been blessed and are obligated to bless others.

After the woman explained to the people how this man told her all about herself, they began paying attention to what she had to say. Not only were they interested, they wanted to see for themselves if what she was saying was true.

A woman who had been devalued by her peers and her community had become valuable to them. God can take an outcast and make others have to rely on that person!

Won't He do it?

CHAPTER NINE

PASSING IT ON

One of the things I love about worshipping with other Christians is hearing them testify about the goodness of the Lord. When a person shares their testimony, you may hear a variety of things. It's possible that you can relate to some of what you hear. In addition, hearing a person's testimony may help you deal with or resolve a situation of your own.

The Samaritans seemed to become receptive of the woman's testimony. Listening to her testimony peaked their curiosity. They decided it was time for them to meet Jesus. Once they went to meet him, they were able to encounter Him for themselves. Not wanting Him to leave, they asked Him to stay. He obliged them and stayed with them for two days (John 4: 39-40). Yes, the woman's testimony got the ball rolling. However, the people investigated things for themselves.

I used to have a thousand different reasons why I didn't believe people when they testified. People would talk about being delivered from this and that. I thought that a lot of people were being too fanatical. Maybe some of them were but who was I to judge anyone? I had no idea what they had gone through to come to believe in God for His goodness and their breakthrough. I was so obsessed with discrediting others that I missed out on what God had for me.

When I looked to the left criticizing Susie's testimony, I missed what God had for me on the right. The reason I was missing out on what God had for me was because I was *meddling* with what God was doing in the lives of others. He didn't need me to observe other people. He certainly didn't need my help.

What He needed me to do was one thing – stay focused on Him! Wow! Whether they were right, wrong, weak or strong – whatever the case may be – other people's testimonies were *none of my business!* Why?

First, we're all human beings. Due to our imperfect nature, human beings tend to fail you. The second reason is our focus needs to be on the *message* and not the *messenger*. "If I had known that Pastor wasn't preaching today, I would have stayed home." "There's nothing she can say that I want to hear." "I can't relate to what he's saying – he's too young (or too old)." Those are a few examples of taking the messenger's inventory. Yet, we receive exactly what God intended for us to receive when we focus on what we should be focused on – the message.

Contrary to my own beliefs, I found myself with a testimony. I was ready to tell the whole world about what God had done for me. Sometimes I got so excited about testifying that I could hardly sit still. When I used to see people take off running in the church, I used to think they had lost their natural mind. Once I discovered my new relationship with God, I felt like running through the church with them. It took some years and maturity for me to understand why people were getting so excited but thank God, I got there.

The two days the Samaritan citizens spent with Jesus proved to be monumental. More of them became believers. They had their own personal experiences with Christ. They shared with the Samaritan woman that they now believe, not just because of her testimony, but because they know it for themselves that He is really the Savior of the world (John 4:41 – 42).

The woman's testimony served its purpose. She told her story to others about her encounter with Christ. She told them the Good News of being delivered from her sins and restored into a new person. It was not her responsibility to make the citizens become believers. They had to decide for themselves. Once they came to Christ, then they had the same responsibility to tell the Good News.

As long as they kept sharing, *The Good News Express* kept going. They were spreading the Gospel on foot by word of mouth. Today, we have countless means to spread the Gospel. With all the means and methods of communication at our disposal, the Good News Express is nonstop. Anytime, anyplace and by any means, we can share the Good News and we can share about The Living Water. We have no excuse not to!

We are supposed to tell others that at one time we were just an old, retched empty bucket. Then we are supposed to give Him the glory by sharing how He poured into us His Living Water, which guarantees we will *thirst no more!*

CHAPTER TEN

HE'S MORE THAN "SOMETHING"

How many times a day do you say "something told me?" Think about it. I say it a lot. "Something told me to close the door." "Something told me not to leave yet."

I monitored myself one day to see how many times I used that statement. I had used the statement "Something told me" at least eight times that day. I found it interesting to see how a few words had become part of my everyday language. I asked myself what was "something?" Then I thought maybe the better question is who "something?"

I believe in God. I am not confused about that

neither do I have any reservations. Until recently, I had not been paying attention to how I was expressing my belief in God. I believe that God loves me, guides me and protects me. But beforehand, I said that "Something told me…" Sounds contradictory, doesn't it? I think so.

As a little girl, Psalms 23 taught me that "Thou (the Lord) art with me" (verse 4). As I grew older, I resented my life. I rebelled against my mother. So many things had happened. I stopped believing that the Lord was with me. I decided to do whatever I wanted to do. I was clueless about the consequences that came with those decisions. At that moment and time, I didn't care about any consequences. As a matter of fact, I stopped caring about anything and everything.

By the age of 12, I had "slipped into darkness," I had crossed over into a dark side of life that I would reside in for the next 19 years. I drank alcohol and used drugs in the dark. I had unprotected sex in the dark. I hung out with hip, slick and cool people in the dark. I became a teenage mother in the dark. I thought it was fun in the dark. I thought it was safe in the dark. I thought I was happy in the dark. People hurt me in the dark. I cried in the dark. My heart broke in the dark. I found myself alone in the dark.

I wanted to come back to the light. I missed the light. I was happy in the light. Life was easier in the light. I wanted to ask for help. I was too ashamed. I couldn't swallow my pride. I didn't want to tell anyone how dark my life was. I didn't have the courage. I thought I was gone to the point of no return. So I hid out in the dark. I convinced myself that I was going to die in the dark.

I lacked light and water. Spiritually, I was dying. My physical death wasn't far behind. I got sick and tired of being sick and tired. I was trapped in the dark. I could not bring myself into light. No human power could relieve me from the dark.

I cried out that three-worded prayer: "God help me!" He sent His Son, Jesus Christ, who told me *my life story!* He didn't care about my past. He only cared about me right then at that moment.

He told me that it wasn't too late. I decided to trust Him. I repented and He forgave me of my sins. He filled *my empty bucket* with His Living Water so I haven't had to *thirst anymore!* His Living Water gave me light.

From that day to this day, I have not been thirsty nor lived in darkness. In His Word, God says that: "*I am the light of the world. Whoever follows me will never walk in darkness, but will have the light of life.*" (John 8:12).

I cannot refer to the power of the Almighty as merely "something." A power like that is more than something! Thank you, Jesus! You are everything! I praise Your name right now!

Your bucket never has to be empty again! Come to Jesus and receive His Living Water. He promises once you receive the Living Water, "it will become in him a well of water springing up to eternal life." (John 4:14)

You don't have to take my word for it – try Him for yourself!

Yvette Wilson Bentley

A Samaritan Woman Meets Her Messiah
John 4:1-42 (New King James Version)

1 Therefore, when the Lord knew that the Pharisees had heard that Jesus made and baptized more disciples than John

2 (though Jesus Himself did not baptize, but His disciples),

3 He left Judea and departed again to Galilee.

4 But He needed to go through Samaria.

5 So He came to a city of Samaria which is called Sychar, near the plot of ground that Jacob gave to his son Joseph.

6 Now Jacob's well was there. Jesus therefore, being wearied from *His* journey, sat thus by the well. It was about the sixth hour.

⁷ A woman of Samaria came to draw water. Jesus said to her, "Give Me a drink."

⁸ For His disciples had gone away into the city to buy food.

⁹ Then the woman of Samaria said to Him, "How is it that You, being a Jew, ask a drink from me, a Samaritan woman?" For Jews have no dealings with Samaritans.

¹⁰ Jesus answered and said to her, "If you knew the gift of God, and who it is who says to you, 'Give Me a drink,' you would have asked Him, and He would have given you living water."

¹¹ The woman said to Him, "Sir, You have nothing to draw with, and the well is deep. Where then do You get that living water?

¹² Are You greater than our father Jacob, who gave us the well, and drank from it himself, as well as his sons and his livestock?"

¹³ Jesus answered and said to her, "Whoever drinks of this water will thirst again,

¹⁴ but whoever drinks of the water that I shall give him will never thirst. But the water that I shall give him will become in him a fountain of water springing up into everlasting life."

¹⁵ The woman said to Him, "Sir, give me this water, that I may not thirst, nor come here to draw."

¹⁶ Jesus said to her, "Go, call your husband, and come here."

¹⁷ The woman answered and said, "I have no husband." Jesus said to her, "You have well said, 'I have no husband,'

¹⁸ for you have had five husbands, and the one whom you now have is not your husband; in that you spoke truly."

[19] The woman said to Him, "Sir, I perceive that You are a prophet.

[20] Our fathers worshiped on this mountain, and you *Jews* say that in Jerusalem is the place where one ought to worship."

[21] Jesus said to her, "Woman, believe Me, the hour is coming when you will neither on this mountain, nor in Jerusalem, worship the Father.

[22] You worship what you do not know; we know what we worship, for salvation is of the Jews.

[23] But the hour is coming, and now is, when the true worshipers will worship the Father in spirit and truth; for the Father is seeking such to worship Him.

[24] God *is* Spirit, and those who worship Him must worship in spirit and truth."

²⁵ The woman said to Him, "I know that Messiah is coming" (who is called Christ). "When He comes, He will tell us all things."

²⁶ Jesus said to her, "I who speak to you am *He.*"

²⁸ The woman then left her waterpot, went her way into the city, and said to the men, ²⁹ "Come, see a Man who told me all things that I ever did. Could this be the Christ?" ³⁰ Then they went out of the city and came to Him.

³¹ In the meantime His disciples urged Him, saying, "Rabbi, eat."

³² But He said to them, "I have food to eat of which you do not know."

³³ Therefore the disciples said to one another, "Has anyone brought Him *anything* to eat?"

³⁴ Jesus said to them, "My food is to do the will of Him who sent Me, and to finish His work.

³⁵ Do you not say, 'There are still four months and *then* comes the harvest'? Behold, I say to you, lift up your eyes and look at the fields, for they are already white for harvest!

³⁶ And he who reaps receives wages, and gathers fruit for eternal life, that both he who sows and he who reaps may rejoice together.

³⁷ For in this the saying is true: 'One sows and another reaps.'

³⁸ I sent you to reap that for which you have not labored; others have labored, and you have entered into their labors."

³⁹ And many of the Samaritans of that city believed in Him because of the word of the woman who testified, "He told me all that I *ever* did."

⁴⁰ So when the Samaritans had come to Him, they urged Him to stay with them; and He stayed there two days.

⁴¹ And many more believed because of His own word.

⁴² Then they said to the woman, "Now we believe, not because of what you said, for we ourselves have heard *Him* and we know that this is indeed the Christ,[a] the Savior of the world."

Yvette Wilson Bentley

Connection Through Reflection

A 30-Day Journey to Habit Formation

No matter where you are on your spiritual journey, it's good to set aside time with God. It's beneficial to reflect on your relationship with Him. It's also a time to achieve a greater and deeper connection.

Taking time to reflect is a great time for self-examination. It is also a great time to begin trusting your mind, heart and spirit with God.

For the next 30 days, I invite you to take an intentional journey. The journey will be with just you and God. Feel free to create your own intentions and outcomes. Here are a few to help you get started:

1. What I can receive from God?

2. What I can give to God?

3. What I will gain if I am willing to change?

4. What will I lose if I stay the same?

5. How I will feel if I do this?

6. How I will feel if I don't do this?

It is my belief and experience that putting pen to paper is a very powerful, yet humbling experience. Writing it down allows you to capture it "in the raw." There's no backspace, no cut/paste. It allows you to see yourself for who you are.

If you don't own a journal, a college-ruled notebook and a writing instrument of your choice will start you on your way. By the end of your 30 days, you will have gained clarity of new spiritual habits and how you would like to implement into your daily routine.

Thirst No More

Thirst No More

Thirst No More

Thirst No More

Thirst No More

Thirst No More

Thirst No More

Thirst No More

Thirst No More

Yvette Wilson Bentley

Thirst No More

Thirst No More

Thirst No More

Yvette Wilson Bentley

Thirst No More

Thirst No More

Thirst No More

Thirst No More

Yvette Wilson Bentley

ABOUT THE AUTHOR

A native of Louisville, KY, Yvette Wilson Bentley has always enjoyed creative writing. It wasn't until recent years that she decided to pursue an active career as an author. ENHANCING THE JOURNEY was Yvette's freshman publication in 2012. Yvette became an avid learner and embraced each component of the publishing process which has solidified her as an author as well as a literary entrepreneur.

Yvette founded her own publishing company, *Wryte Type Publishing* in 2014 and is scheduled to print her first publication, "Thirst No More: A

Woman's Journey to Restoration" in February 2015.

Yvette holds memberships in The Sisters of Ruth Book Club and the M-Pact Writers Group. She has been a contributing writer for numerous newsletters and local magazines. She has also been a featured guest on a number of internet radio shows, including "Inspirational Talk With Toneal," "Awakened Internet Radio" and "Jerry Royce Live!"

Yvette also hosts a monthly talk-show, "Candid Conversations," where she headlines a variety of self-help topics and engages both a guest and her audience in transparent conversations. In addition, Yvette is a public speaker, workshop facilitator and life coach who has a passion for connecting with women that are seeking restoration in their lives from past and current life and spiritual issues.

In her spare time, Yvette enjoys reading, bowling, traveling and relaxing with friends and extended family members.

CONTACT INFORMATION

For more information, order additional books, or to schedule speaking engagements, teleseminars, webinars, book club or group meetings:

www.ywilsonbentley.com
Website

info@ywilsonbentley.com
Email

www.facebook.com/YvetteWilsonBentley
Facebook

www.ywilsonbentley.com/thejourney
Blog

@ynb65 on Twitter

@ynb65 on Instagram

www.ingramcontent.com/pod-product-compliance
Lightning Source LLC
Chambersburg PA
CBHW072055290426
44110CB00014B/1691